TABLE OF CONTENTS

P9-EMQ-937

CHAPTER ONE

THAT GOLDEN GLOW

What makes a good friend? Would you want a friend that's smart, outgoing, and playful? Should a friend also be loyal and true? If you think so, I've got the perfect friend for you. It's a dog with winning warmth and limitless love. This dog has a golden personality. It's a golden retriever!

The Gorgeous Golden

Golden retrievers are often called goldens for short. Their name comes from the color of their coats. Goldens come in all shades of gold.

Above: These goldens range in color from pale gold to reddish gold.

GREAT NAMES FOR YOUR GOLDEN

Your dog should have a super name. Do any of these fit your golden retriever?

Moondog

Goldie   Frisbee   Gypsy   Sunny

Dazzler   LYRIC   Sandy

BUDDY

CHEWBACCA

These dogs aren't small. Males range from 23 to 24 inches (58 to 61 centimeters) high at the shoulder. Put two 12-inch (30 cm) rulers together. You'll see how tall a golden is.

Some people think that goldens are the perfect size for hugging!

A male dog weighs between 65 and 75 pounds (29 to 34 kilograms). That's about as much as seven large house cats. Female goldens are a little smaller than males.

QUITE A COAT

Goldens stay warm in the winter. They have a double coat. This means they have two layers of fur. And water doesn't stick to their fur. If your golden gets wet in the rain or snow, it won't stay wet for long.

A Fun-Loving Friend

Goldens have lots of energy and like to have fun. They also love being with their owners. Your golden will go hiking and jogging with you. These dogs are also great swimmers. They'll have a super time with you in a lake or a pool.

Some people say that a golden's feelings show on its face. These dogs always seem to be smiling. Their owners think they are the best dogs ever. It's not hard to see why.

WHITE HOUSE PET

A golden once lived in the White House. President Gerald R. Ford had a golden named Liberty, pictured at left with President Ford and his daughter, Susan, in 1974. White House guests enjoyed seeing this playful pet.

Golden retrievers love to run. Try to keep up!

CHAPTER TWO

THROUGH THE YEARS

Goldens got their start in Scotland. In the late 1800s, they served as hunting dogs for the rich. Their owners liked to shoot birds for sport. Yet these men didn't care to fetch the downed birds. They used dogs for that. Goldens went through the mud and weeds to bring back the birds.

Goldens Get Around

Later, people took these dogs to England. They also brought the dogs to the United States, Canada, and other places. People saw that goldens were more than good hunting dogs. They also made great family pets.

This British couple takes three golden retrievers out to hunt in 1938.

These days, the American Kennel Club (AKC) groups dogs by breed. Some of the AKC's groups include the toy group, the hound group, and the working group. Goldens are in the sporting group. Dogs in the sporting group are active, alert, and likable. Many are also good hunting dogs.

This Afghan hound is in the hound group.

Yorkshire terriers are in the toy group.

This boxer belongs to the working group.

Ready, Willing, and Able

Like all sporting dogs, goldens are loyal and hardworking. In modern times, these dogs do many different jobs. Some are guide dogs for the blind and people who do not see well.

Goldens can also be trained to help a person in a wheelchair. They can learn to get items off high shelves. These dogs can pick up dropped items as well.

Top: This golden retriever is a guide dog. It helps its owner across the street.
Bottom: Golden retrievers can be trained as service dogs. This golden is helping its owner grocery shop.

This golden retriever is training as a rescue dog. It practices digging someone out of the snow.

Other goldens are search and rescue dogs. They look for people who are missing or hurt. Sometimes, they search for days at a time.

A DOG NAMED BEAR

Bear was a golden retriever that helped after the World Trade Center in New York City was destroyed in attacks on September 11, 2001. He searched for people who were trapped beneath the World Trade Center's rubble. Bear put in eighteen-hour days at the Trade Center site. When he died in 2002, hundreds of people came to a special service for him.

Bear gets water from his owner after searching at the World Trade Center site in 2001.

A GREAT GOLDEN DOG

Doc is a golden ski patrol dog and a true hero. Ski patrol dogs help to find skiers who are lost, trapped, or hurt in the snow. Doc dug out a skier buried under 5 feet (1.5 meters) of snow. Doc saved the skier's life.

Still other goldens are therapy dogs. These dogs are brought to hospitals and nursing homes. They cheer up people staying there.

Golden retrievers are easy to admire. You can depend on them to do a job or just to be a good friend.

Golden retrievers can get along with every member of the family—even cats!

CHAPTER THREE

THE RIGHT DOG FOR YOU?

Golden retrievers have real appeal. But don't rush out to get one. Is a golden really right for you? Read on to see.

Goldens on the Go

Goldens are high-energy dogs. They need lots of exercise.
Would you rather watch TV than play outside? Do you plan to put
your dog in the backyard instead of walking it? If so, you might
be better off with a gerbil or a cat.

Goldens need room to move around and stretch out. Do you live in a small apartment in a large city? Are there few parks or open spaces nearby? If so, a smaller dog might be a better choice.

A Beautiful Coat, but . . .

Goldens have beautiful coats. Yet these dogs shed a lot. If you have a golden, you'll need a good vacuum. Expect to find dog hair on your clothes, furniture, and floor.

19

A People Lovin' Pooch

Goldens want to be around people. They will enjoy going camping, swimming, or hiking with you and your family. A golden left alone all day will be an unhappy dog. It may develop behavior problems.

Goldens need lots of exercise. They will enjoy going for walks or swimming.

Do you have time to exercise and play with a dog? Is your family ready to accept a large, furry new member with lots of energy? Think about these things before getting a golden.

NOT A GREAT WATCHDOG

If you need a good watchdog, don't get a golden. They usually don't bark at strangers. What if someone broke into your home? Don't count on your golden to scare off the robber. These dogs would want the thief to pet them or play with them.

Do you still want a golden? You're lucky if it's the right dog for you. Your new canine is sure to bring you many hours of good company, fun, and love.

AS THE YEARS PASS

Most golden retrievers live for ten to twelve years. As they grow older, these dogs show signs of aging. You'll see gray hairs on the dog's face and body. By the age of nine or ten, your golden will have less energy too. You might have to be extra loving and patient with your loyal pet.

CHAPTER FOUR

BRINGING YOUR DOG HOME

Getting a dog is always exciting. You are getting a new best friend. You want the big day to go smoothly. There are some things you can do to make that happen.

Plan Ahead

Plan to stay home the day your dog arrives. Your pooch has a lot to get used to. Make your new dog feel at home.

These golden retriever puppies will grow fast. Soon they'll be ready for training.

You'll need supplies for your pet. Below is a list of some basics to help you get started:

- collar

- leash

- tags (for identification)

- dog food

- food and water bowls

- crates (one for when your pet travels by car and one for it to rest in at home)

- treats (to be used in training)

- toys

Training your golden retriever will take time and patience.

SAFETY FIRST

Keep your golden in a crate for car rides. A dog loose in the car can be hurt during sudden turns and stops. A crate will also protect your dog if there's an accident. It's up to you to keep your golden safe.

Need a Vet? You Bet!

You'll need to take your new dog to a veterinarian soon. A veterinarian, or vet, is a doctor who treats animals. A vet will help keep your dog well.

The vet will check your pet's health. Your dog will also get the shots it needs. You'll be taking your dog back to the vet for checkups and more shots. And be sure to take your dog to the vet if it gets sick.

Time to Eat

Give your dog love and attention. But don't give it table scraps. Dogs need to eat dog food. Ask your vet which food is best for your dog. Don't use dog treats as dessert for your pet either. Give your dog treats only as rewards in training. You want your pet to stay lean and healthy.

Put out a bowl of cool water for your dog. Change this water a few times a day. And be sure to keep your dog's bowls clean.

Golden Time Together

Your golden will bring you years of smiles and joy. You'll grow up together. Your dog will always be there for you.

PLAY WITH YOUR POOCH!

Goldens were bred to fetch birds. These dogs love playing fetch with their owners. Toss a ball or a Frisbee to your dog. You'll both have a great time.

In turn, you must be there for your dog. Remember that a dog is a living thing. Be sure to give your dog the love and care it needs. Your golden retriever will be your best friend. Be its best friend as well.

Giving your golden baths and grooming its thick coat is important. This helps keep your dog clean and healthy.

GLOSSARY

American Kennel Club (AKC): an organization that groups dogs by breed. The AKC also defines the characteristics of different breeds.

breed: a particular type of dog. Dogs of the same breed have the same body shape and general features. *Breed* can also refer to producing puppies.

canine: a dog; having to do with dogs

coat: a dog's fur

guide dog: a dog trained to lead people who do not see well or are blind

search and rescue dog: a dog trained to find people who are injured or missing

shed: to lose fur

sporting group: a group of dogs that tend to be active and alert. Dogs in the sporting group make good hunters.

therapy dog: a dog brought to nursing homes or hospitals to comfort patients

veterinarian: a doctor who treats animals. Veterinarians are called vets for short.

FOR MORE INFORMATION

Books

Brecke, Nicole, and Patricia M. Stockland. *Dogs You Can Draw.* Minneapolis: Millbrook Press, 2010. This colorful book teaches readers how to draw different kinds of dogs, including the golden retriever, and shares fun facts about each breed.

Gray, Susan H. *Golden Retrievers.* Chanhassen, MN: Child's World, 2007. Read this book to learn more about golden retrievers.

Landau, Elaine. *Your Pet Dog.* Rev. ed. New York: Children's Press, 2007. This title is a good guide for young people on choosing and caring for a dog.

Markle, Sandra. *Animal Heroes: True Rescue Stories.* Minneapolis: Millbrook Press, 2009. Markle tells how dogs, cats, monkeys, and other animals have saved humans from dangerous situations.

Patent, Dorothy Hinshaw. *The Right Dog for the Job: Ira's Path from Service Dog to Guide Dog.* New York: Walker & Company, 2004. Read this book to learn the true story of how a golden retriever named Ira was trained as a guide dog.

Websites

American Kennel Club

http://www.akc.org

Visit this website to find a complete listing of AKC-registered dog breeds, including the golden retriever. This site also features fun printable activities for kids.

ASPCA Animaland

http://www2.aspca.org/site/PageServer?pagename=kids_pc_home

Check out this website for helpful hints on caring for a dog and other pets.

Index

Photo Acknowledgments

The images in this book are used with the permission of: backgrounds: © iStockphoto.com/Julie Fisher and © iStockphoto.com/Tomasz Adamczyk; © iStockphoto.com/Michael Balderas, p. 1; © age fotostock/SuperStock, pp. 4, 19, 28, 29; © Eric Isselée/Dreamstime.com, p. 5; © Jerry Shulman/SuperStock, pp. 5 (inset), 12 (bottom right), 22 (bottom), 28 (inset); © iStockphoto.com/Paul Kline, p. 6; © Mark Raycroft/Minden Pictures, pp. 7 (top), 25 (bottom); © Karen Kennedy/Dreamstime.com, p. 7 (bottom); © Cohen/Ostrow/Digital Vision/Getty Images, p. 8; AP Photo, p. 9 (top); © iStockphoto.com/sonyae, p. 9 (bottom); © Vgm/Dreamstime.com, p. 10; © Davis/Hulton Archive/Getty Images, pp. 10-11; © Kwame Zikomo/SuperStock, p. 11; © iStockphoto.com/Eric Isselée, p. 12 (top left); © Jszg005/Dreamstime.com, p. 12 (bottom left); © Peter Skinner/Photo Researchers, Inc., p. 13 (top); © Nadia Borowski/San Diego Union Tribune/ZUMA Press, p. 13 (bottom); © Lezlie Sterling/The Sacramento Bee/ZUMA Press, p. 14 (top); AP Photo/Beth A. Keiser, File, p. 14 (bottom); © iStockphoto.com/iofoto, p. 15; © Mitja Mladkovic/Dreamstime.com, p. 16 (top); © iStockphoto.com/Aldo Murillo, p. 16 (bottom); © Pixbilder/Dreamstime.com, p. 17; © Mike Neale/Dreamstime.com, p. 18; © Cheryl Clegg/SuperStock, pp. 18-19; © Temelko Temelkov/Dreamstime.com, p. 20; © Sunheyy/Dreamstime.com, p. 20 (inset); © iStockphoto.com/fury123, pp. 20-21; © Jerry Amster/SuperStock, p. 21; © The Copyright Group/SuperStock, p. 22 (top); © Adriano Bacchella/naturepl.com, p. 23; © Lawrence Migdale/Photo Researchers, Inc., p. 24 (top); © Jane Burton/naturepl.com, p. 24 (bottom); © Tammy Mcallister/Dreamstime.com, p. 25 (top); © April Turner/Dreamstime.com, p. 25 (second from top); © iStockphoto.com/orix3, p. 25 (second from bottom); © Joe Sohm/Visions of America/Photodisc/Getty Images, p. 26 (top); © GK Hart/Vikki Hart/Taxi/Getty Images, p. 26 (bottom); © Brand X Pictures/Getty Images, p. 27; © Richard Hutchings/Digital Light Source/Peter Arnold, Inc., pp. 28-29.

Front cover: © GK Hart/Vikki Hart/Photodisc/Getty Images.
Back cover: © iStockphoto.com/Phil Date.